THE EMERGING
Christian Woman

SHE BRINGS UNITY & VITALITY
TO THE BODY OF CHRIST

Anne Gimenez

Creation  House
Altamonte Springs, Florida

First printing, April 1986
Second printing, September 1986

All Scripture references King James Version
unless otherwise noted.

Creation House
190 N. Westmonte Drive
Altamonte Springs, FL 32714

To Christian women everywhere
who hear Christ's call to use
their gifts to bring vitality
and peace to the church.

CONTENTS

Foreword..9

1   God's Plan for Balance...13

2   Esther's Story..21

3   Women Then...and Now...35

4   Women in New Testament Days.....................................45

5   Single-mindedness..57

6   Encouragement Not Competition....................................69

7   Wholeness...79

8   Women Restored...93

Afterword..101

Recommended Reading...105

FOREWORD

A veil is parting—a brand new day is opening before us. The light that is breaking will reveal the secret weapon God has been holding back until this very hour. What is that secret weapon? *Women.*

For centuries, women have been kept down, stepped on, owned and left behind. Even today, Christian leaders put forward the idea that Eve brought a curse on all women and that women are still under a curse. But could it be that God, in His desire that all things be "reconciled to Himself," is working out a higher plan?

Yes, He is! And many are catching a glimpse of it. Today, Christian women are stepping out of the Dark Ages of rejection. We are searching to find our place in the body of Christ. The church is awakening, discovering that in its midst are women who are gifted, trained, called to leadership roles. We are a virtually untapped treasury of teachers, administrators, speakers. Old walls are being shaken, broken down.

Never has it been more crucial that godly women step

forward and accept their place beside men in the church. Feminists have been trying for several decades to destroy womanhood, manhood, the home and the church. This is the hour when Christian women, empowered by the Holy Spirit, can rise up and stand against the destructive forces that would destroy us all.

Yet some would ask, "What are you saying? Women in *leadership*? Aren't women supposed to be quiet? Aren't they supposed to stay in their place? Aren't you going against the Bible?"

For years I struggled with those very questions—struggled with the "call" I felt upon my own life, knowing I would be going against the grain. But like a needle drawn to a magnet, I could not deny the force of that call. Timidly, I stepped out. I met resistance—and I met the power of God. As I learned to be obedient, He has led me, comforted me and confirmed His work for me. I could ask for no greater mark of approval than His.

Women continually come to me, wondering, "What can *we* do in the body of Christ?" I love to tell them, "Anything God calls you to!"

That's right. And that call is not just a supernatural thing—not only an indefinite "feeling" inside. His plan for women is revealed, I believe, in His Word. For years, I have searched the Scriptures to discover God's plan for women—and what a plan it is!

I believe God is restoring His church today. As He does, women will be restored to their rightful place. And restored women are the key to the restoration of manhood. In the words of the apostle Paul, it is the godly women who will lift up the man, "notice, regard, honor, prefer, venerate and esteem him" (Eph. 5:33, Amplified).

That's why I believe we are standing on one of the most exciting threshholds in history. As God moves women into their rightful place, a new unity will come between man and woman. In the marketplace, in the church, in marriages, strife will end.

I have been told that all of this sounds a little prophetic, like a dream of the future. I used to think so too. In those days, as a woman, I had a lot of frustration. Maybe you know what that's like. But God's plan is unfolding right now. Do you want to discover it, as I did?

Then read on....

Chapter ONE

GOD'S PLAN FOR BALANCE

I slipped on jeans and an old work shirt and quickly ran a comb through my hair. My usual Saturday housework awaited me. I had to attend to a thousand details before tomorrow's worship service. "It's going to be a full day," I sighed, catching a glimpse of my appearance in the mirror.

I paused before the mirror. Was I ready for this day? I thought.

My husband, John, had been traveling six days a week for months, making plans for Washington for Jesus, a major rally which several hundred thousand people were expected to attend. He was downstairs at the breakfast table now, and he would probably have a dozen questions for me: What songs will the choir be singing tomorrow? What happened at the elders' meeting? Have you arranged for next week's guest speaker? We are co-pastors of a 5,000-member church; our agendas are sometimes staggering. Since John was away so much of the time, I found myself saddled with many of the church responsibilities—besides running the household and keeping up with our very active daughter, Robin.

I smiled at my reflection, certain I had covered everything and was ready to answer John's questions efficiently.

Efficient? Is that what I felt? My smile faded slightly. No, it was something else. Something was wrong. But I didn't have the time today to ponder for long the feeling that had been slowly twisting inside for weeks— maybe longer.

Instead, I plunged down the stairs and hurried into the kitchen. John was sipping coffee in the breakfast nook. He had been up early, had gone out for a short jog and was now scanning the local paper.

I can't remember what he said that lit the fuse. Maybe he had asked a question about the one thing I had forgotten to do. I was amazed at how short the fuse was and how great the explosion. Suddenly a fury of words spewed out of me. The twisting feeling, the thing that had gotten "under my skin," worked its way out. If I'd been able to think rationally at that moment, I would have recognized it as full-blown *resentment.* But I wasn't acting or thinking rationally. John sat wide-eyed, his coffee mug half-way to his lips.

I stomped up the stairs and fled to the bedroom. I tore back the bedcovers, got in and pulled the sheet over my head. It must have been quite a funny sight for John, who had followed me up the stairs. There I lay, a woman in her 40s, crying in bed with a sheet over her head. I had never done anything like this in my life. Half of me was embarrassed; the other half enjoyed settling down into a good pout.

John is the sort of man who is generally in command,

and normally I snap-to when he gives an order. "Anne Gimenez!" he now demanded. "Get out from under those covers—right now!"

"I will *not*!" I shot back, pulling the sheet even tighter.

"Then at least tell me what's wrong!"

I could detect a slight note of desperation in John's voice. Perhaps he thought I'd gone over the brink. Even I was amazed at the words that spilled out.

"It's—it's *everything*! I'm expected to be a wife—and a good one. I'm expected to be a mother—and a good one. And there's everything else." I listed all the other things I was expected to be good at: being a pastor, counseling, teaching the Bible, leading worship.

Somehow John calmed me down and coaxed me out from under the covers. Sheepishly, I followed him downstairs, where, over coffee, he assured me of how needed I was, how hard it would be for him to try to manage without me—in short, all the things he thought I needed to hear. I thought I needed to hear those things too. They made it possible to keep moving through the day.

But I soon realized that something else was at the root of my discontent. I was tired of feeling like a second-class citizen. When this thought first occurred to me, I was alarmed.

Did I resent John's authority over me as a husband? I could honestly say I did not. John always kept a good balance between "chief of the Gimenez tribe" and "chief servant." He has a loving authority that makes submission easy for both Robin and me. And even though he and I are "co-pastors," I've made it plain that he is really the leader of the flock.

The truth was that I felt that my work wasn't as important as John's. Much was asked of me, and I was comfortable and confident doing whatever was required. My work wasn't *un*important. It was just not *as* important as the work of a man.

I was feeling something that many women experience. If a woman is a good teacher, some will think of the Bible study she organizes as a "lonely hearts" group. If a woman reaches out to help the poor or hurting in our society, some will think she doesn't have enough housework to keep her busy. A highly skilled woman can organize the office files, juggle a man's tangled appointment calendar, see that the financial books are kept in order, and still be referred to as "his gal Friday."

I wasn't sliding into the camp of the secular feminists—those women who are trying to un-sex both men and women and destroy God-ordered lines of authority. But something is wrong with the way women are viewed, even by the church. It is a second-class status, the kind of thing that's expressed with unthinking glibness in the remark I've often heard about our mother, Eve: "After all, she bit the apple first."

In the weeks following my Saturday morning explosion, I found myself wondering what Eve was doing *before* the fall. Was there another way to view women, besides the traditional view the church has taken throughout the years?

With those questions in mind, I opened my Bible to Genesis one evening and read the familiar story of creation. In the glow of the bedside lamp, I let the words sink in, especially the part about the creation of Adam and Eve.

So God created man in his own image, in the image of God created he him; male and female created he them. And God blessed them, and said unto them, Be fruitful, and multiply, and replenish the earth, and subdue it; and have dominion over the fish of the sea, and over the fowl of the air, and over every living thing that moveth upon the earth.

(Gen. 1:27-28)

For the first time, a key word stood out for me: the simple little word *them*. God told *them*—the man and the woman—to have dominion, or lordship, over everything on earth! Eve was not just Adam's "side-kick," as I had sometimes thought. She didn't trudge through the garden, broom in hand, sweeping up after the animals while he exercised his authority. They were created to rule together—to exercise power and authority jointly!

This thought stirred me greatly. I felt a surge of excitement at my first glimpse of the role Eve had been created to fulfill. I noticed that even Adam, seeing Eve for the first time, exclaimed, "This is now bone of my bones, and flesh of my flesh" (Gen. 2:23). There were no divisions for Adam; Eve was, to him, another *self*.

I read on in Genesis—to the fall of Eve, Adam's fall and finally God's curse. How many times had I heard women told that they were now to be completely in subjection to men, because of the curse? On the basis of this one Scripture passage, women have been told they have no right to any leadership position whatsoever.

But hasn't the curse been lifted? I mused. John and I, like so many thousands of others across the world, have entered into the renewing life of the Holy Spirit. We have been learning how the Spirit has been restoring to God's children all the covenant rights that mankind lost through the fall. The death of Jesus Christ restores us to fellowship with the Father; the Holy Spirit is empowering us to do His work on earth. As God's Spirit sweeps through the church, we are regaining more and more authority over every evil thing—over sickness, poverty, ignorance and wickedness. In fact, we often referred to this outpouring of power as "the full gospel."

I realized it was half the gospel. Somehow—and I include myself—we had been proclaiming that, in Jesus, the curse was lifted and dominion restored *for men.*

I asked: Has the curse not been lifted, in Jesus, for women as well? Can we enjoy full co-dominion in God's order? Can we be the leaders God first intended us to be?

If restoring women to leadership roles was truly God's plan, then I knew there must be an unbroken train throughout the Bible that revealed and confirmed this plan. Re-reading Genesis that evening was just an initial spark that set me afire with interest, and I began searching the Scriptures.

I was amazed at what I discovered. I found freedom from many inner struggles and from so many resentments. I found myself excited and challenged with a new knowledge about my role as a woman in God's kingdom. I found relationships clarified: no longer was I confused about my relationship to my husband and other authorities, nor was I confused about my own giftedness and God-ordained calling.

Since that time I have talked with thousands of other women who are struggling with what it *means* to be a woman in God's kingdom. Many have been put down, stepped on, trodden by legalistic bondages—never glimpsing the tremendous role they are supposed to be playing as the Holy Spirit prepares the church for Jesus Christ's return. Their bondage is the work of Satan, who has been an enemy of women since Eden. If you are a woman, then Satan is *your* enemy.

But I have good news! We have entered a new era, a time when the light of God's truth is breaking through the dark barriers that bound women for centuries. And it is not just for the few or the select.

My prayer is that you will find in these pages the keys that will restore to you the dominion—the place of balanced authority—that God intended.

After all, it has been His plan all along.

Chapter
TWO

ESTHER'S STORY

Many women in the Bible are often praised for their exceptional faith. Tens of thousands of sermons have been preached about Sarah, Hannah and Ruth and their ability to believe God. Yet I suspect that most of those sermons make one of two lessons: the importance of being a godly, praying mother, and the fact that their obedience to the word of God brought forth godly sons.

Both of those lessons are very important. But less often do we hear messages from pulpits about women like Deborah, who was a judge in ancient Israel. Of course, little is really known about Deborah. There is another Old Testament woman whose story is remarkable, not because she was in the lineage of the Messiah or bore another godly son, but because God placed her in a crucial position at a crucial time.

Her name is Esther. I learned much from the story of Esther as I began my search through the Bible for women God had chosen for leadership roles.

It is hard for American women of the 20th century to understand how women were treated in Esther's day. In the culture of the Middle East, women were considered property. A woman's parents usually chose her husband. Her husband often had several wives, for even in the Hebrew culture, a man's worth was measured by how many heads of cattle and how many wives he had. A woman could be divorced by her husband and sent away from her home and children if he so chose. The woman's responsibility was to bear sons for her husband. Women who were barren or who bore only daughters shamed their husbands and were social outcasts. Women were not numbered among the tribes of Israel, nor were they included in genealogies. They were next to nothing. In short, they suffered beneath a terrible weight.

Even worse, in Esther's day—around 400 B.C.—most of the people of Israel had been carried away captive into Babylon. The Hebrew men, women and children were all slaves. If a Babylonian man wanted a Hebrew woman, he could take her away from her people entirely and make her his wife.

This is what happened to Esther, an orphan girl who was raised by her older cousin, Mordecai. Esther struck it rich. She found favor in the eyes of the great King Ahasuerus, also known as Xerxes I. The king was powerful; he ruled over 127 provinces from India to Ethiopia, a huge part of the known world at that time. He ruled with an iron fist from his palace in Shushan, the capital of his empire.

The one thing the king did not rule was the heart of his first wife, Queen Vashti. Vashti offended the king and paid the price.

King Ahasuerus prepared a giant feast to celebrate his reign and invited all his nobles and princes and servants. On the seventh day of the feast, when the men's hearts were "merry with wine," this powerful king issued a seemingly simple order. He told his servants to "bring Vashti the queen before the king with the crown royal, to shew the people and the princes her beauty: for she was fair to look on" (verse 11).

But Vashti was having the ancient equivalent of an ERA rally. Her response to the king shows that her heart was rebellious. She was having her own party—on his expense account—with a group of Persian women. When her husband summoned her to honor him, she *dis*honored him before all his men by saying she was too busy to come.

Vashti violated one basic principle: You are never too busy for a king!

This was not only a personal offense to the king. It was a potential crisis in the kingdom, as the king's messengers explained to him: "For this deed of the queen shall come abroad unto all women, so that they shall despise their husbands in their eyes....Thus shall there arise too much contempt and wrath" (verses 17-18).

Now the king was faced with a serious problem. His wife's action could upset every household in the kingdom because she had diminished the king in the sight of everyone. Not surprisingly, the king banished Vashti and the other rebellious women from the land.

Vashti's spirit is in the world today, destroying marriages, homes and families. Everywhere, women are upsetting God's order by asserting themselves over their husbands. Little wonder that our society is poised on the verge of disintegration, for "a false balance is abomination to the Lord, but a just weight is his delight" (Prov. 11:1).

In recent years, men and women have been rediscovering biblical principles for marriage and the home, yet in our human way, we have gone overboard with a certain principle. For a long time, women were supposed to be in abject submission, with little or no voice in the church. Now, however, many Christian women have taken the opposite approach, even usurping their husband's place in the home. Many homes have gone from one unbalanced position to the other.

And yet many women are trying to find the balance. They honestly want a godly, balanced home life, have talents and gifts and callings to fulfill, but do not want to overthrow their husbands and pastors. What should they do?

This is where Esther enters the picture.

King Ahasuerus needed a queen to replace Vashti. He proceeded wisely. He sent his men through all the provinces to gather the fair virgins of the land. Mordecai, who had reared Esther as his own daughter, brought her to see the king also.

The choosing of a new queen was a long process. Each woman had to submit to 12 months of purification before the king set eyes on her! For Esther, who believed in the living God, this was more than a ritual cleansing—it was certainly a time when God was purifying her. During this time, she "obtained favor in the sight of all them that looked upon her," including the king's chamberlain, his right-hand man (Esth. 2:15). It would not be hard to imagine that all his servants and counselors were continually telling the king about this extraordinary woman who brought a special grace and peace to the palace. Undoubtedly, this was part of the king's test; surely a wise king would want to know the character of the woman who would reign with him. In fact, Esther met the king years after Vashti had left.

So, with all that he had heard about her, the king summoned Esther into his throne room at last: "And the king loved Esther above all women, and she obtained grace and favor in his sight more than all the virgins; so that he set the royal crown upon her head..." (verse 17).

Two things are important about Esther's becoming queen.

Esther was first purified. The word *purify* means to rid something of polluting or corrupting elements—to free from sin and guilt. In the plan God had for her, this was absolutely necessary. He wanted to be sure that she had none of the attitudes of Vashti because He had an assignment for Esther that a brazen woman could never handle. Through her time of waiting, Esther proved her patience and inner beauty before both God and the king.

That made possible the second step. Ahasuerus *made her queen*. Esther could not have proclaimed herself queen. The king did it. God's order is in this. A woman does not have to argue for or insist upon her place of leadership in God's kingdom. In fact, the more she yells and complains and demands, the more she proves that the time of purification is not finished. Any ministry that is ordained by God—whether the ministry of a man or a woman—will always be recognized by others. In Esther's case, her new husband placed the crown on her head.

One minor but important fact fits in here. Mordecai had the good sense to give Esther a small bit of advice, something like this: "Whatever you do, don't talk about your relatives. Leave your family out of it!" Undoubtedly, this was one reason Esther and the king had a happy marriage! In any case, Esther did not say anything about the fact that she was a Hebrew.

And so five years later, Esther found herself in a remarkable position at one of the most desperate moments in Hebrew history to that time.

Haman came upon the scene—and he hated the Hebrews. Evidently, he was a proud, egotistical man who demanded that everyone bow when he made his entrance. In this way, he had made himself a false god, like Satan. The Hebrews, who had been commanded by God not to bow before any false gods, resented Haman. A powder keg was waiting to explode.

The man who touched off the fuse was Mordecai. The king recognized him as a man of wisdom, and Mordecai was given the right to sit "in the king's gate," which meant that he was in a place of some governmental power. He had even warned Esther about a plot to kill the king, and so the would-be assassins were hanged. He had proven himself loyal to the king, but he would not bow to the devilish Haman.

Haman decided to have Mordecai hanged as a traitor too. He not only convinced the king that the man who had saved his life was himself a traitor, but Haman also convinced him to sentence every Hebrew in the land to death! With the king's ring in hand, the symbol of power, he set the awful machinery in motion. Letters were posted to the king's military throughout the empire. In a few days, without warning, every Hebrew man, woman and child was to be brutally murdered.

When word of this decree reached Mordecai, he put on sackcloth and ashes and went to the gate to fast, pray, weep and mourn. He told Esther about Haman's decree and begged her to go into the king's inner court and plead for her people. He was saying, "Now is the time, Esther. Now you must make yourself vulnerable—and reveal who you really are."

Esther responded like so many of us: She panicked. She got legalistic. She replied to Mordecai by quoting a law:

All the king's servants...do know, that whosoever, whether man or woman, shall come unto the king into the inner court, who is not called, there is one law of his to put him to death, except such to whom the king shall hold out the golden sceptre, that he may live: but I have not been called to come in unto the king these thirty days.   (Esth. 4:11)

In short, Esther said, "Not me. Sorry, but I can't do it. Besides, a woman can't be given such responsibilities!" But Mordecai quickly reminded her that surely she would be found out as a Hebrew too.

Think not with thyself that thou shalt escape in the king's house, more than all the Jews. For if thou altogether holdest thy peace at this time, then shall there enlargement and deliverance arise to the Jews from another place; but thou and thy father's house shall be destroyed: *and who knoweth whether thou art come to the kingdom for such a time as this?*
                    (verses 13-14, italics added)

What an incredibly faith-filled reply. Mordecai believed that God would find some way to rescue His people. He always had. It just seemed natural to Mordecai that God had not allowed Esther her position as queen for no reason at all, but because she was called upon to touch the innermost recesses of the king's heart on God's behalf. God was about to use her, not because of her looks or charm but because He had spent years investing in her character. He called forth that investment now.

Esther told Mordecai to gather all the Jews in the capital city of Shushan to fast and pray for three days. She would gather her handmaidens and they, too, would fast and pray. In other words, she said, "Before I presume anything, I am going to get on my knees and touch God."

We Christian women must learn to react like that. Often we don't.

Any woman called into a leadership role has a natural tendency to be fearful. Perhaps that's because we sense—as Esther seems to have sensed about the satanic Haman—the nature of our evil adversary, the one who has hated us from the beginning. We also need to act like Esther and get on our knees and build a personal rapport with the Lord. Our ministries don't depend on promotion, publicity, books, records, personal beauty or television programs. Our ministries depend on our connection with God and His anointing upon us. We need to be women who will turn to God in prayer and then do whatever He asks of us.

That's what Esther did. She listened to God and found out that He really was calling her. Now she was ready to put her throne, her kingdom and her very life on the line.

On the third day of the fast, she put on her royal apparel and went to the king's inner court. What she did seems a simple thing, but she was violating her husband's law. At a word from his lips, she could be put to death if he thought she was acting presumptuously by coming to his seat of power.

But when Ahasuerus saw Esther, he extended his sceptre to her. That small act said much. For many years, this woman had honored him as her king and her husband. Had she been a fussing, brawling, contentious woman, he might have said, "Now's my chance! Take her away to the dungeon, boys!" But he was not about to take off the head of the woman who had made him happy.

Every man deserves to be king in the eyes of his wife. If a woman makes her husband king, then she will be queen. We have to be careful how we treat our husbands and how we talk about them. If I say my husband is a "bum," then I am the wife of a bum, for I am his other half. Some women show disrespect to their husbands for years and wonder why their husbands have no respect for them. Similarly, some women criticize their pastors and elders for every petty reason they can think of, and then wonder why their ministries or opinions are not accepted.

Esther's husband recognized her in the fullest sense. When he called her to his side, it is obvious that he was overcome with love for her. For he said, "What wilt thou, queen Esther? and what is thy request? It shall be given thee to the half of my kingdom" (Esth. 5:3).

Notice that he did not offer her more than half the kingdom, for had she taken it, she would have had more authority than he. And that would have constituted an imbalance in their relationship.

Esther did not make her request at once, but told the

king that she was throwing a party in his honor the very next evening. (And whose money do you think she spent to put on this party?) Haman was invited, too.

At this party, in the presence of her enemy and the enemy of all her people, Esther made herself most vulnerable to her husband. She did not put Ahasuerus' reputation on the line as Vashti had. Nor did she say, "Okay, pal, you promised me half the kingdom. So hand it over, and I'll go live there with the rest of my Jewish people." Again, she honored him. "If I have found favor in thy sight, O king, and if it please the king, let my life be given me at my petition, and my people at my request" (Esth. 7:3).

He granted her request and spared the Hebrew people. The king must have cherished Esther above his own kingdom, because granting her request meant rescinding an order he had already issued bearing the seal of his ring. He was risking having his nobles say, "Look at her. He's letting his wife run the show." But that did not occur to the king, because he overthrew Haman's plot and had Haman hanged on his own gallows.

And so, through a woman, the Hebrews were saved from annihilation.

Three important lessons about women in leadership stand out from Esther's story.

First, Esther humbled herself and went through a time of purification. She admitted she was unclean. When she did that, God worked within her. God Himself made her ready.

Some women today act aggressive, arguing for their "rights," displacing men, grabbing for leadership. There are Christian women who have the same heart attitude as the toughest, most pushy, secular businesswomen. We want our rights! Yet the Bible says, "Humble yourselves, therefore, under the mighty hand of God, that he may exalt you in due time" (1 Pet. 5:6). Humbling, not demanding, is always the first step in the process of becoming a leader.

Second, Esther gained favor through the humility and grace that God was building into her character. She did not force herself into the king's household saying, "Do it my way, or else. Because I may be the next queen around here and heads will roll." She became queen because of the good report the servants gave about her. Most especially, she continued to submit to the king. Even in the direst situation, she did not conspire behind his back or manipulate.

This thought caused me some embarrassment. More than once I have listened to a Christian sister knock her pastor because she has received some direction from the Lord that he was not ready to hear, and then she goes out behind his back to get things done "for the Lord." How many times have I heard a woman cutting down her husband for his "lack of spirituality"? But who was really lacking? Like Esther, we must still respect and submit to the authority over us—for a king is a king is a king!

Third, perhaps the most beautiful lesson from Esther's life was the very natural way God had arranged all the events. After all, in His sovereignty, it was He who allowed her to be carried into captivity and to be wed to the king. In short, she simply led a godly life, and "God exalted her in due time." The word is *relinquishment*. "Let go and let God." However you want to express it, He is still the best arranger of events and lives that I know.

As I finished my study of Esther, I had to admit that she was thrown into some very unusual circumstances. Was she really God's example of what a woman in leadership could accomplish? Or was she an oddity? My interest was burning, and I was drawn next to the Old Testament prophets.

What I learned there both stunned and thrilled me.

Chapter
THREE

WOMEN THEN... AND NOW

A woman's lot in Old Testament times was not a good one. Few women enjoyed privileges; only queens like Esther had any influence. It seemed to me that women were almost like captives. They were held in spiritual and cultural bondage. Women were strictly governed under Hebrew law. Because women were always having to purify themselves after their monthly cycles, and after the birth of a child, meant that they were almost always in a state of uncleanness. If we women think we wrestle with self-image today, imagine how a young Hebrew woman in Old Testament times felt! These restrictions on women were brought together in the Talmud, a collection of authoritative opinions and interpretations of Scripture that evolved by the end of the Old Testament period.

At some point, God began a mighty work to bring women to the position of relative freedom they enjoy today.

It was with these thoughts in mind that I rediscovered

a familiar passage in Ezekiel:

The hand of the Lord was upon me, and carried
me out in the spirit of the Lord, and set me down
in the midst of the valley which was full of bones,
and caused me to pass by them round about: and,
behold, there were very many in the open valley;
and lo, they were very dry. And he said unto me,
Son of man, can these bones live?

(Ezek. 37:1-3)

There had been life; now there was only evidence of
death and desolation. And in the midst of it, God was
asking, "Can there be life here?" I could imagine
Ezekiel shaking his head.

That scene made me think at once of a similar passage
in Isaiah: "This is a people robbed and spoiled; they
are all of them snared in holes, and they are hid in prison
houses; they are for a prey, and none delivereth; for
a spoil, and none saith, Restore" (Is. 42:22).

Both prophets are describing people who had been
robbed and spoiled until they felt that there was nothing
left but dry bones scattered in the dust. These passages
have always been interpreted as referring to God's
restoration of the nation of Israel.

But they could also be viewed from a fuller New
Testament position. For we know now that God restores
all things and every person to their rightful place in
Christ Jesus. Satan wants to keep down and destroy;
God wants to heal and restore.

I thought again of Eve—of Adam's joy when he first
set eyes on her. "This is now bone of my bones," he
said, "and flesh of my flesh" (Gen. 2:23). I believe
he was also glad that he would have someone to rule
the earth with him. But Eve turned from God, and in-

stead of life, she received the sentence of death. She became a dry bone and carried women into the bondage of legalism and traditionalism for centuries after.

Even my own experience had proved that. I recalled a painful time when, as a young woman, I had begun to answer God's sovereign call upon my life. From the outset, the power of tradition had been against me.

When I was growing up, it was not popular in my part of Texas to be Pentecostal. Because my family wanted no part of these "holy roller" churches, my only exposure to the workings of the Holy Spirit was through an aunt I visited once a year. But as a young girl, I felt a deep stirring within me, the call to preach the gospel.

This call stayed with me even though I was a rebellious teenager. I hung around with a tough crowd, smoked and carried a switchblade in my purse. But I recall telling one boyfriend, "Some day, I don't know how it will ever happen, and I don't know if I'll be gray-headed and creakin' on a cane, but I'm going to preach the gospel." He nearly swallowed the cigarette he was smoking.

Not long after that, when I was 17, I went to a tent meeting where Gordon and Freda Lindsay were preaching with Daisy and T. L. Osborne. I received the baptism in the Holy Spirit and God's call to preach the Word.

I began attending Pentecostal churches regularly. Although these churches were certainly open to the move of God's Spirit, it was there, like Esther, that I experienced my first painful "purification." It came through a bit of legalism and traditionalism.

My home church had about 400 members—large for a Pentecostal church in the 1950s. I had been speaking at many smaller churches where pastors seemed to recognize my calling to preach. I had even led week-long revival meetings. One day my own pastor mentioned casually that I ought to be prepared to give a week's worth of sermons in our church. I was nearly spinning with joy! After speaking in so many little tar-paper and board-sided churches, I wanted nothing so much as to bring God's Word to my own home fellowship—before 400 people!

For weeks I fasted and prayed and searched my Bible, until I knew God had given me something from Him for these people.

But weeks went by before the pastor mentioned it again. Finally, one day he said to me, almost off-handedly, "Oh, by the way, why don't you get your messages together and be ready to preach a few weeks from now. We'll start on a Sunday evening and you can preach for the whole week."

On Sunday morning, the day I was to begin, the pastor stopped me after Sunday school and, in the same off-handed manner, said, "By the way, Anne, did you really have your heart set on preaching this week?" Before I could answer, he said, "My son-in-law is an evangelist, and he and my daughter came home last night. They need a week of meetings to fill their schedule. So you won't mind if they preach this week, will you?"

I was crushed. I wanted to preach in my own church so bad I could taste it. I fought back tears. I had always been taught to respect authority, and all I could manage to say was, "Whatever you think is best. You are the pastor."

The worship service was beginning and there was no time for further discussion. I led the worship singing as usual. Then I took my seat in the congregation—that morning I sat up against a wall so no one could see the red-rimmed eyes behind my Bible—and the pastor came to the podium. Unthinkingly, he proceeded to deal me the worst blow of all.

"Well, folks," he began, "Sister Anne was going to preach to us this coming week, but I guess she won't be doing that. I don't know why. I guess she doesn't have enough messages." Around the sanctuary, people began to chuckle. And the pastor was laughing, too, as he announced who the "surprise" speaker would be.

But I had turned my face to the wall so that no one could see the burning tears that poured down my cheeks. Perhaps the pastor meant it as a joke, but at the moment, I could only feel the cruelty. Silently, I prayed, *Give me something, God. I'm hurting so bad and I need You right now.*

I looked down through the tears at the Bible as it had flopped open in my lap. Unbelievably, it had fallen open to 1 Peter, where it says to humble yourself under the mighty hand of God and He will exalt you in His time.

Sitting in that pew, I vowed that I would forgive my pastor, that I would put a smile on my face and lead songs for the pastor's son-in-law and let God take care of the hurt in my heart. And I did. And He did.

Years later I recognized that what had happened to me happened in the context of the way women are treated even in the church. Even though the church is made up mostly of women, the men are in charge. Many women are trampled upon and put down, their feelings bruised or discounted. God never intended this. Unfortunately, it has become a traditional posture of the church to deny women leadership, overlooking their

God-given callings to their deep detriment and to the great loss of the body of Christ. And it is sometimes done with callous disregard, even with the mentality that it is a service to God to put women down and under.

The oppression continued, even after John and I had been called by God to co-pastor the Rock Church in Virginia Beach, Virginia. Preachers would gladly answer an invitation to speak from our pulpit, but it was only John ("please, *just* John") whom they invited to speak in their churches. Finally John objected to these brothers' preaching in a church where a woman was co-pastor while denying a woman's calling to bring forth the Word of God. At times I begged John to let me step aside so the attacks would stop. But in his wisdom, John refused. I was his rib, bone of his bones, he said, called of God to lead with him. He seemed to know in the Spirit that a day of restoration was coming.

These experiences, plus what I was learning from Scripture, were the context in which I read the passage in Ezekiel. Beyond the restoration of Israel, beyond the restoration of God's Spirit to His body the church, I now saw another restoration in motion. Now I could hear God's voice speaking directly to women: "Prophesy unto these bones, and say unto them, O ye dry bones, hear the word of the Lord" (verse 4).

The word *dry* in this passage means free from moisture, not giving milk—and at once I could relate that to women. Dry also means uninteresting, sarcastic, plain, void of ideas. I realized that this described me sometimes, as well as many other women I knew. It was as if someone pulled the plug on the women of the church and drained all the life away. Without life, you cannot give life. In struggling for a living identity, Chris-

41

tian women have copied the world and copied men. We have competed and pushed and clawed. But that is wrong. God was saying to me through this passage that He would restore women to their first estate in the pattern He had intended.

Ezekiel goes on: "So I prophesied as I was commanded: and as I prophesied, there was a noise, and behold a shaking, and the bones came together, bone to his bone" (verse 7).

Something powerful and supernatural happened! The word *shake* means to move with quick vibrations, to tremble, a severe shock, to shake off and get rid of. God seemed to be saying He would make a time when women could shake off the yoke of tradition and legalism. The Scripture said, "Bone to his bone." When God restored women to their right place in the body, it would be in right relationship to men—not above men or below them, but side by side as God intended.

Ezekiel continued: "And when I beheld, lo, the sinews and the flesh came upon them, and the skin covered them above" (verse 8).

Now these resurrected bodies had some form. This was the position women had come into. Women are encouraged to develop their talents and skills. The Christian marketplace seems to be flooded with books for women, encouraging us to develop our self-image and feel good about ourselves. But God wants more than that, as the prophet made plain:

But there was no breath in them. Then said he unto me, prophesy unto the wind, prophesy, son of man, and say to the wind, Thus saith the Lord God; Come from the four winds, O breath, and breathe upon these slain, that they may live (verse 8-9).

The word "slain" is significant. The dead who lay there had been deliberately slain by a calculated action. Since God was talking about spiritual death, He was talking about Satan—the enemy of women, the one who brought us death and continues to fight to keep us dead. It is he who is the enemy, not an unsaved or domineering husband or a tradition-bound pastor.

Nevertheless, God is calling women out of spiritual death into life—and power! "And I shall put my spirit in you, and ye shall live" (verse 14).

Shall live! Not just dragging along, like an afterthought, always bringing up the rear, but alive with God's Spirit.

Other prophecies openly proclaim the restoration of women in God's kingdom. Consider Joel's stirring vision of God's creative, restorative work:

And it shall come to pass afterward, that I will pour out my spirit upon all flesh; and your sons and your *daughters* shall prophesy, your old men shall dream dreams, your young men shall see visions: and also upon the servants and upon the *handmaids* in those days will I pour out my spirit.

(Joel 2:28-29, italics added)

Reading these remarkable words, I felt super-charged. And I was bursting with even more questions.

When would this full restoration take place? When would we begin to hear the rattle of bones—and see men and women coming together to hold dominion side by side in the body of Christ? When would God's mighty Spirit blow life back into the spirit of women, ending Satan's oppression?

It was with this excitement that I turned to the New Testament.

Chapter FOUR

WOMEN IN NEW TESTAMENT DAYS

Joel 2 is an important link to the New Testament. Man had lost the Spirit of God within. A major part of God's plan through the ages was to make a way for His Spirit to dwell inside us once again so we could enjoy His presence as He longs to enjoy ours. Joel prophesied a time when the Spirit and fellowship and power would again be available to the people of God. When Peter quoted that prophecy, as recorded in Acts 2, the Old Testament promises were at last being fulfilled.

Of course I was eager to jump to Acts 2 because I knew that Peter, in quoting Joel, would talk about daughters who would prophesy—that is, speak forth the word of God. But since too many people pull a scripture here and a passage there and come up with a new doctrine that's unbalanced or off completely, I first re-read the Gospels to see how Jesus interacted with women and to see what role they played in His life and ministry.

Some people say that Jesus didn't change a thing in

regard to the place women hold. "After all," they argue, "all the apostles were men."

But consider the roles women played in His ministry. In Luke's Gospel, I was touched by the account of Mary's visit to her cousin Elizabeth. It is not clear when this visit took place, but perhaps it was during the tense time when Joseph had heard the unsettling news that his wife-to-be was already expecting and he was thinking of quietly ending their betrothal. In any case, Mary must have needed human encouragement. She received it from Elizabeth, who comforted her with joy and compassion:

...and Elizabeth was filled with the Holy Ghost: And she spake out with a loud voice, and said, Blessed art thou among women, and blessed is the fruit of thy womb. And whence is this to me, that the mother of *my Lord* should come to me?

(Luke 1:41-43, italics added)

God filled Elizabeth with His Spirit and gave her divine revelation which she spoke out, not sweetly or demurely, but in "a loud voice."

Nor was Elizabeth the only woman God used prophetically in Jesus' early life. When Mary and Joseph presented the child Jesus in the temple to be dedicated and circumcised, they were greeted by the prophetess Anna. Anna had been married seven years when her husband died. She then took up residence in the temple courts, fasting, praying and serving God night and day. Considering her great love for God and her constant attention to Him, it seems only natural that she should minister prophetically, speaking the things she knew to be in His heart. When God's only Son came to be dedicated, Anna, of course, His prophetess, was there:

"[Anna] coming in that instant gave thanks likewise unto the Lord, and spake of him to all who looked for redemption in Jerusalem" (Luke 2:38).

Anna announced that salvation had come. It is significant that God chose a woman, not a priest or a male teacher of the law, to express the joy in His heart on that day.

Things got even more interesting when I began reading about the start of Jesus' public ministry. For Jesus had come to abolish the curse, to make all things new again and to reconcile all things to God. (See 2 Cor. 5:17-19.)

Jesus' encounter with the Samaritan woman at the well was a major event, a time when Jesus stepped outside the customs of the day to make a point. John, who recorded it, was not present for the conversation. He must have had to dig out the facts later in order to write about it. What so impressed John and the others about this encounter?

I read: "And upon this came his disciples, and *marvelled that he talked to the woman*" (John 4:27, italics added).

Since men were the influential ones in Israel, the disciples wondered why on earth Jesus was wasting His time talking to a woman. How could she further His ministry? How could she further this "kingdom" they hoped to reign in as Jesus' righthand men?

But Jesus took the time to deliver a pressing message to the Samaritan woman: The hour had come for her to forsake her sinful life and open herself to the Holy Spirit along with everyone else who was hungering for God. God was about to pour out His Spirit again on all flesh, male and female. What a startling revelation for a woman to hear after so many centuries of spiritual dryness!

The most intriguing encounter between Jesus and a woman involved Mary Magdalene, the woman who went to the garden tomb to finish the ceremonial preparation of Jesus' body.

Jesus had cast seven demons out of Mary Magdalene. (See Mark 16:9-11). Tradition has it that she was also a prostitute. Certainly she was a woman who had been trapped in satanic darkness. She had suffered from the curse. She had been abused and mistreated by men for their pleasure. And yet something amazing happened when she went to the garden on that first Easter morning.

The first and mightiest thing, of course, is that the body of Jesus was gone. Mary Magdalene and the disciples saw that. Later they realized that Jesus had risen from the dead and showed Himself as the risen Lord. But look at how this discovery came about.

Peter and John gave up looking for Jesus' body and went home. So did the other women who went to the tomb with Mary Magdalene. But she stayed behind, weeping, not willing to give up her search for Him. She was rewarded, for Jesus suddenly revealed Himself to her, and she fell lovingly at her Master's feet. I felt at once that all women were rewarded in her persistence.

Why did Jesus wait until only Mary remained in the garden to reveal Himself? Why did He not appear a few minutes earlier, when His beloved friends Peter and John would have been there to rejoice?

It is only speculation, but it seemed to me that, as Jesus was the second Adam, perhaps Mary Magdalene represented Eve. She had certainly suffered from the curse enough. Jesus had just closed the long-open gap between man and God; perhaps His next act was to close the gap between man and woman. By honoring Mary Magdalene in this way, perhaps He was re-establishing woman's place of co-dominion there in another garden.

If that is speculation, what happened soon after certainly is not. In the book of Acts, we see how Peter, newly swept with the fire of the Holy Spirit, stood before a crowd of Jews and quoted the prophet Joel. It was the beginning of a new age of fulfillment. Men *and women* would prophesy, filled to overflowing with God's Spirit. People should not be surprised at signs and wonders. They should be ready to receive the word of the Lord from young and old, men and women. What a glorious new day!

Acts 2 says that 120 disciples were gathered together in one place and, moreover, they were in one accord. The 11 remaining apostles were there, along with Mary the mother of Jesus and the other women and men who had followed Jesus. Unexpectedly, the sound of a mighty rushing wind filled the house where they were, and tongues as of fire fell upon them and each one began to speak in a new language proclaiming the word of God—what we refer to today as the gift of other tongues.

The news of what was happening spread fast, and a huge crowd of people who were living in Jerusalem gathered in the street to find out what was going on. The 120 were preaching to this crowd. Peter saw the shocked expression on the faces of the people of the city, and he stood up to address them. I was surprised at what he said. He did not say what you would expect: "Do you hear what's going on? These people are speaking in other tongues! It's a miracle!"

Under the power of the Holy Spirit, he quoted Joel

2, where the prophet speaks of a time, a new day in God's calendar, when God's Spirit would fall upon both men and women and "sons and daughters" would prophesy.

Peter was saying, "The miracle is not that we are speaking in tongues so much as that God has reinstated women into their rightful place in His kingdom's service." Women were non-persons in this day and age. They did not count; when a census was taken, only the men 20 years of age and older were counted. Some even debated whether or not women had souls. With a few exceptions, like the prophetess Anna, they certainly were not allowed to speak out the Word of God in public!

What joy I felt when I realized this fact: With the sacrificial death of Jesus, the curse was broken and Satan's oppressive hold over women was ended; the day of Pentecost was God's way of publicly proclaiming that freedom.

Peter was not the only New Testament man to recognize that women were no longer to be kept down. I read this in Paul's letter to the Galatians:

For ye are all the children of God by faith in Christ Jesus. For as many of you as have been baptized into Christ have put on Christ. There is neither Jew nor Greek, there is neither bond nor free, *there is neither male nor female:* for ye are all one in Christ Jesus. And if ye be Christ's, then are ye Abraham's seed, and heirs according to the promise."

(Gal. 3:26-29, italics added)

Paul echoes Peter in telling believers that there is no excuse for discriminating against a person because of nationality, social standing, or *gender*.

However, certain portions of Paul's letters have been

quoted out of context and used as "proof texts" against women in ministry.

I could not count the number of times I had finished preaching or teaching, only to be faced at the end of the service by a brother with a serious look and an open Bible in his hand.

"Sister Gimenez," the brother would begin.

I'd think, Here it comes. Then I'd politely short-circuit the attack.

"You've come to ask me what I think about 1 Corinthians chapters 11 and 14, right?"

Surprised, he would nod.

I have discussed these scriptures with noted Bible scholars and knowledgeable preachers. This is how I understand them. Take 1 Corinthians 11:3: "But I would have you know, that the head of every man is Christ; and the head of the woman is the man; and the head of Christ is God."

My brother would be amazed to find that I have no trouble with that scripture whatsoever. God established this order for the sake of our society and the peace of the home. Some Christians today think the husband and wife should both be leaders in the home. But anything with two heads is a freak. In our home, I tell our daughter Robin that Daddy is the boss—and believe me, he is. When Daddy is not there, I'm the boss. She has authority over the dog. That's the way it goes.

But then, my brother asks, "What about the fact that you preach and teach?"

We look at 1 Corinthians 14:34-35:

Let your women keep silence in the churches: for it is not permitted unto them to speak; but they are commanded to be under obedience, as also saith the law. And if they will learn anything, let them ask their husbands at home.

We must put this passage in its context. First of all, the Corinthian church was in terrible disorder. There were reports of incest. The people were divided into factions. In the first part of chapter 14, Paul corrects misuse of the spiritual gifts. Tongues are to be used publicly only when there is an interpreter. If none is present, those with a message in tongues are to be silent. Likewise with prophecy; if there is no one to judge the prophecy, then the prophet should be silent.

Then Paul takes up the matter of women speaking in church. He doesn't say women were preaching or teaching; he says they were not being silent. In the early churches, which were modeled after the synagogues of that time, men sat on one side and women sat on the other. Paul was dealing with the fact that women were calling out to their husbands across the church as if they were in a Greek marketplace where they were used to hearing philosophical dialogues while they shopped and chatted. Paul says, "If you want to *learn* anything, be quiet."

Another passage often quoted to me is 1 Timothy 2:12: "But I suffer not a woman to teach, nor to usurp authority over the man."

However, there are two Greek words that are translated "man" in English. One means members of the male sex. But the Greek word here is *aner*, which means "husband." Paul is telling wives not to usurp their husbands' authority.

Indeed Paul recognized Aquila *and* Priscilla as leaders of a local church. He entrusted Phoebe to deliver his letter to the Romans. Likewise, the apostle John wrote his second letter to "the elect lady," encouraging her to stand against deceivers, warning her to have discernment about those who came to meet in her home.

I found Paul's seemingly negative position not to be negative at all. In fact, I found it to be perfectly in line with Peter's later teaching in his first letter:

...ye wives, be in subjection to your own husbands...Likewise, ye husbands, dwell with them (your wives) according to knowledge, giving honor unto the wife, as unto the weaker vessel, as being heirs together of the grace of life, that your prayers be not hindered.   (1 Pet. 3:1,7)

This scripture seems to make three points.

First, women are told to be in subjection to their husbands. Certainly that goes along with what we know about God's order for the home. This goes along with Paul's teaching. But notice that it says nothing about women's role in the church. If a woman is a strong leader, people automatically wink at each other and say, "We know who wears the pants in that family!" That is wrong. A woman can be a strong leader *outside* the home, as long as she is under the authority of her husband when she is *in* the home.

Second, the passage says that the wife is the "weaker vessel." That troubled me at first. Some women are not the "weaker vessel" emotionally, spiritually or even physically. What Peter is saying here is simply that in the home, the wife has less authority.

Third, and most important, the husband is told to honor his wife "as being heirs together of the grace of life, that your prayers be not hindered." Again, this goes along with Paul's message to the Galatians. It says, "In God's kingdom, women are equal. They have co-dominion as joint heirs with Christ. If a man does not recognize this, does not honor the woman God has put in his life, he may find that his prayers have little power.''

By the time I finished my New Testament survey, I felt that I was bursting with a new treasure. I was elated when I thought about the women who had influenced Jesus' early life and of Mary Magdalene, whom He had honored after His resurrection.

In fact, Mary Magdalene held even more special interest for me. Tradition has it that she never married but left Israel and carried the gospel north to Russia. A huge, beautiful church stands on the slopes of the Mount of Olives now near the Garden of Gethsemane honoring her missionary zeal.

For years, I had remained single also—so long in fact that I nearly despaired of ever marrying. Yet it was during those years that I came to know God as my ''husband'' and provider. As I trusted in Him, I found that He guided me, cared for me. Because I was unencumbered by the cares of a family, He led me into His service in a way I would never have imagined.

With those thoughts in mind, I turned my attention and my studies to the place of the single woman in God's kingdom.

Chapter
FIVE

SINGLE-
MINDEDNESS

A t this point in my studies, I felt as though I were standing on the long, flat ribbon of history. The past was behind, the future ahead. Looking to the past, I could see some of the effects of Eve's enmity with the serpent. Every woman who has been called to a leadership role stands the chance of facing rejection, having the validity of her ministry questioned, and loneliness.

Loneliness! How well I knew loneliness. I recalled my days as a single woman, on my own and past 30, serving God and longing for a man to share my life with. For me, loneliness was one of the greatest struggles of all. Yet I had learned so much about the special place of ministry that God has for a single woman—and all the lessons and dangers that go along with that calling.

I don't remember how I received my call to preach. Some children want to be a nurse or a fireman, but as far back as I can remember, I wanted to preach. That was quite unusual, because my family was not very religious and I had never seen a woman preacher. Though I went my own way for a little while as a teenager, it seems that God never forgot.

When I was 17 years old an unusual thing happened as I was attending some special services in a little Pentecostal church in Corpus Christi, Texas. The people leading the services came back to where I was sitting and asked if they could pray for me. The word of the Lord came to them, and they prophesied out loud that I would stand before multitudes and preach the gospel.

After the service, my pastor, Garlon Pemberton, asked me, "Did you know you were called to preach?" And sheepishly I said, "Yes."

But first God had to train me.

Shortly thereafter, I found myself living away from home with nothing to my name but a car and the contents of my purse. I was president of the young people's group, and many Friday nights I would preach during our fellowship time. About that time, another young woman and I made plans to go into the ministry and travel together.

One day, my friend left for a short trip. The next day, I received shocking news: She had been killed in an accident.

I was devastated. Immediately I thought, That's the end. I can't go into ministry now. But God showed me that I had become dependent on this woman and that I needed to push ahead with Him. And with His comfort, I did.

I expected to launch into a traveling ministry right away. I was surprised that God had more training in mind.

There had been some serious strains and tensions between me and my parents. The Lord made it clear to me that I was not to go *out*, but to go *home*. I heard Him say, *I'll tell you when to leave.*

So I did. For eight and a half years I lived at home and worked for a large company as an accountant. During these years, my dad came into a personal relationship with Christ, which thrilled me tremendously. At work, I was promoted and became head of my department. Still I waited for that call of God, wondering if I was on some enormous side-track.

But the important thing was that I didn't sit around waiting for the call that would place me "before multitudes." I did the small things. All during those years, I took any invitation to preach, no matter how small the group, no matter how far I'd have to go to get there. This was my ministerial training, for God never led me to go to a Bible school.

Finally, the call came again. A church in Houston asked me to become its youth minister, and they would give me liberty to travel and preach revival meetings. Just when I had achieved success in my career and was receiving a comfortable salary, it was time to leave all that and head out. I had learned much in the eight-and-a-half years at home. I had learned how to manage money, how to work well with people and how to get by on my own.

But the one thing I hadn't quite learned to manage was loneliness.

Now I wasn't looking for a man under every bush. But when I left my company to enter the ministry in April 1963, I was already 30 years old. Something about that age makes a single woman swallow hard. It hadn't troubled me too much when all my friends got married. But a deep loneliness opened in my heart when they began to have their babies.

The feelings of loneliness were not crippling, but they were hard to escape. As it turned out, I never got to the church in Houston, because God opened up a traveling ministry for me. I ventured throughout the Midwest and into the East, wherever anyone would call me. I bought a little poodle for a traveling companion just to keep from talking to myself.

One evening while I was on the road, I went out to supper with a friend. We were joined by two other older single women who were in ministry. As we sat together over supper, I felt a chill as I watched our two companions. They seemed very masculine, or at least set in their ways. But the worst of it was looking at the four of us. Four old maids, I thought. Silently, I prayed, *God, I don't mind being in the ministry, and I don't mind not being married. But, God, I don't want to be like those two—sort of masculine.*

The worst time of all was a snowy night in Arkansas.

The road was empty, the sky was gray and the land was bleak as I pulled up to a motel. It had small, cheap cabins. I had to be at a meeting in a day or two, so I had time to relax along the way. The man at the desk was not very friendly, but he did carry my overnight bag to the cabin for me. Then he handed me the key— and there I was, alone in a lonely, ice-cold room with my little dog.

We curled up under the covers together, both shaking with the cold and trying to keep warm together. As I lay there in the dark, with only the sound of an occasional truck going by outside to break the silence, I prayed, *Lord, there is not a soul in the world who knows where I am tonight, or even cares.* And with the deep hurt, the tears came.

I had every reason to feel lonely. But then and there I decided that I was not going to sit around and feel that I was missing out on life just because there was not a man beside me. I made a conscious, deliberate decision to be a well-adjusted adult.

Married or single, Lord, whichever way You want it, I prayed. *But I'm not going to live a bitter, self-pitying life.* With that, I was able to sleep.

There was no instant change, but not long after, I met John Gimenez. Almost two years after that, we were married. But the point of the story is not that I eventually got married. What I learned from those years between the time my friend was killed in the car crash and the time I married John was that God wants you to be *single-minded* whether you are single *or* married. If you are single, He wants you to set your face to serve Him no matter what the cost seems to be. If you are married, He wants you to do the same. He is the God of your todays, and He knows what your tomorrows hold.

Young people, and especially single women, have a very hard time these days, because society has really scrambled up our priorities. In the not-too-distant past, most women did not enter their 20s unmarried. Now many women do not even think about marriage until they are in their late 20s, and more women are waiting now until they are in their 30s to begin their families.

There is nothing wrong with this *if* women are delaying marriage and family for the right reasons. I fear they are not. I fear that many young (and not-so-young) single

women are not *single-minded* for God but are career-
minded or material-minded. Men and women of the
post-war "baby boom" years think that a successful,
meaningful, fulfilling life means that they must travel,
be gourmet cooks, wear the latest fashions, own a sports
car and live in a house with a jacuzzi. Then, when
they've got their material lives in order, they are ready
to add one or two children. Then they are ready to let
God get a real foothold in their lives. Too often there
is not much room left for that.

Now I'm not saying that every single (or married)
person who is pursuing a career ought to be doing
something else. But all of us need to be single-minded
toward God, giving Him the first and the best, not just
the rest.

Making God first is our first order of business, for
He has marvelous things in store for our lives.

The second lesson for single women has to do with
those deep dreams we all harbor.

The big dream for many single women is to get married and have a family. But marriage is not happiness.
Happiness is God. There is no other ultimate happiness,
no higher joy in this world. If you believe that sex is
the big mystery, you will find that the mystery ends with
marriage. Sex is very wonderful, but if you get married with the attitude that sex is going to fulfill you,
you'll wake up one day and say, "Is this all there is?
Have I missed something?"

The lesson for all of us, the single woman especially,
is *trust*: "Trust in the Lord with all thine heart; and lean
not unto thine own understanding" (Prov. 3:5).

Trust in the Lord. Confide in the Lord—that is, make
Him your confidant. Depend on the Lord. Rely on and

rest in the integrity of the Lord. Give Him the management and care for your life. For many single women, it is tempting to call on the Lord only when your car breaks down and you're not sure how to fix it. But He wants you to be confident in Him, to rest your present and your future in His hands. Solomon also says, "In all thy ways acknowledge him, and he shall direct thy paths" (Prov. 3:6).

Acknowledge means to recognize. Recognize God in your situation. If you are walking as a single woman, acknowledge that God is with you where you are right now.

This is essential if single women are to lead. Single women often have a hard time accepting God's call to lead because they wrestle with self-esteem. Either they fear that people will not take them seriously, or they feel bad about themselves because they are still single and "incomplete." That is where trust comes in.

If God has called you to lead, *trust* Him. Trust Him to make the way. Trust Him to defend you if others criticize or condemn or oppose you. Trust Him when He says that you are complete in Him. Don't accept the lie that a woman without a husband is only half a person. Meditate on scriptures like Paul's prayer for the Ephesians:

> ...that the God of our Lord Jesus Christ, the Father of glory, may give unto you the spirit of wisdom and revelation in the knowledge of him: The eyes of your understanding being enlightened; that ye may know what is the hope of his calling, and what the riches of the glory of his inheritance in the saints. (Eph. 1:17-18)

You can trust God to do all of this for you as a single

woman. I know. I have walked there.

The third area that single women need to learn about is the danger of leadership roles.

The first danger is entering a ministry for the wrong motives. Some women think, "As soon as I find a husband, I'll ditch what I'm doing for God and lead a normal life." This is a foundationally wrong motive—you should not be involved in a ministry just to kill the time until something better comes along. God does not want us to live in tomorrow; He wants us to live in *today*. Today is when God wants to use us.

The next three words for anyone to learn when moving into a leadership role are: submit, submit, submit.

Some women think they have heard these words so often that they would like to scream. But, with Paul, I say that there is now "neither male nor female." "Submit" is not a sexist word. Everyone in leadership is called to submit.

Anyone who feels he or she has heard a sovereign call from God has to be very careful about ego. This goes for the woman who feels called to preach or speak a prophecy in church or form an intercessory prayer group. Each of us is in danger of polluting God's call with our ego, just as King Saul did in ancient Israel. Saul did not submit his own ego to God's Spirit but raged when he discovered that God had another to take his place. He did not trust God but went to seek out knowledge of the future from the witch of Endor. In other words, he received a sovereign call from God and then did what he liked.

You should submit yourself to your pastor and the elders of your church. When you do that, you are not limiting your freedom but are simply gaining a spiritual covering that you as a single woman need in lieu of a husband's covering. For those who aren't so hifalutin' spiritual, the word covering is also spelled p-r-o-t-e-c-t-i-o-n. All of us need that.

Those of us who have felt called or gifted in a certain way are tempted to act independently and even arrogantly. A prophet will speak out in the Sunday morning worship service whether or not our pastor feels comfortable with that, whether or not he and others have validated our ministry. Paul writes, in 1 Corinthians 14, that if anyone has a message in tongues and there is no interpreter then keep quiet, never mind how *unctioned* you are. I mentioned that to someone once and they said, "But, Sister Anne, I just can't keep quiet." And I said, "Oh, yes, you can. Stuff a handkerchief in your mouth!"

Now what happens when I do submit? Suppose I go to my pastor and tell him I have a call to minister, and he smiles and says, "Fine, we need a teacher for our first-graders"?

The answer is simple and straightforward: Teach the first-graders.

There are no shortcuts in God's kingdom, not if you truly have the call of God on your life. Take your eyes off those who seem to have "made it" to the top in record time. The truth may be that you are coveting their position. Confess that and forsake it. Let God make of your life what He wants it to be; let Him take you by whatever road He wants to take you. The Scriptures say that He will "exalt you in due time." And *all the time* remember that you are an apprentice, a handmaiden of the King of kings.

Finally, be inclusive, not exclusive. If God has called you to establish, let's say, an intercessory prayer ministry, invite your pastor's wife to get involved in leading it if she has a mind to. Keep your pastor informed of what is going on so that he can be alerted to problems that you have become aware of in the body. If you have a prophetic ministry, seek the pastor out and tell him what you are hearing from the Lord. Ask him how to proceed if God seems to be giving you direction. Be willing to accept his guidance. Remember, you are only one part of the body of Christ, not all the arms, the legs and the brains, too!

Regardless of these cautionary words, single women need to remember this: If God has called you and gifted you, never let your self-esteem get in the way, whether it's too low or too high. Do not cheat the body of Christ by holding back, by being afraid to risk or being concerned that others will not recognize your ministry.

If God is calling you to step out of your "comfort zone" and risk for Him, meditate on these words, written by the apostle Paul to a young, unattached person: "Neglect not the gift that is in thee, which was given by prophecy, with the laying on of the hands of the presbytery" (1 Tim. 4:14).

Clearly this verse speaks about the conferring of spiritual authority. But when I meditate on this scripture, I see hands reaching out, touching, not only giving but *receiving*. I see ministry touching ministry, one calling touching another. I see a smooth-working church, the body of Christ. Balance. People working together without tension or strain in unity.

It's a wonderful picture, isn't it? Maybe you think it is impossible, especially if you are a woman who feels that you are bucking the headwinds that would deny— or at least question—your leadership abilities. But the image of a smooth-flowing church is not fantasy. It is God's plan, and He will bring it to pass—but He also requires our cooperation.

How do we, as women called to leadership, take part in God's unfolding plan for the church? How do we help heal the age-old fracture between men and women that has divided the church's power?

The answers I have found can help you bring healing, wholeness and balance—if you will dare to try them.

Chapter
SIX

ENCOURAGEMENT NOT COMPETITION

I t's important to look at some of the practical considerations of a woman's involvement in leadership. The last thing God wants is for women to become involved in warfare against men in resuming co-dominion. We cannot afford more division in the body of Christ.

Let's look at a neglected element in the story of Adam and Eve —their struggle against each other. We don't often think about tension between them, only about their sin against God. But let's look at the record.

Recently, I felt God was speaking a messsage to me: "It is time to put off the reproach of Eve." I had never heard this expression before. I was stumped. What did He mean by that? In searching the Scriptures again, this was what I found.

When the serpent lied to Eve, he promised that she could eat of the fruit and not die—more importantly, that she would become "like God" (Gen. 3:5). As we know, Eve did eat. And what did the serpent say next?

He did *not* say: "Eve, go and find your husband. He's somewhere on the other side of the Garden, just where I knew he'd be so he wouldn't interfere with my tempting you." What went on in Eve's head, now corrupted as a result of her sin? For centuries, theologians have led us to believe Eve was plotting, thinking, Well, as long as I've blown it, I might as well drag my husband down in sin with me. But that's not what she thought.

The Bible says Eve ate, then gave some of the fruit to her husband who was with her. Adam was not deaf, dumb and blind or asleep or off picking strawberries. It appears that he was right there at Eve's side the whole time, listening and hearing everything that was going on between her and the serpent. It's not fair or even accurate to say that Eve's corrupted, sinful, conniving thoughts made her tempt Adam into eating the fruit. For we read that it was after Adam ate that "the eyes of them both were opened" (3:7). They received the knowledge of good and evil when they had sinned *together*.

This story raises another question: *Why* did Adam eat the fruit offered by Eve? She didn't display a sudden god-like power. She didn't tease Adam or tempt him, as some teach. I suggest that *fear* caused Adam to take the fruit in his own hand and eat it. Adam saw that Eve didn't die—at least not the physical, immediate death he was expecting. If not, then maybe Eve *had* become like God, he thought. Maybe she was suddenly *superior* to him. No doubt this would motivate him as nothing else would.

Recently, I heard a gifted Bible teacher speak on this same passage. He pointed out that, in that moment, just after Eve ate of the fruit, Adam was in a crucial position. Since he had not eaten, he could have stood his ground against the serpent's temptation. When God came to walk in the garden again, Adam could have *interceded* for his wife. Perhaps he could have saved her from the effects of her sin, just as Christ, the second Adam, interceded for the church. But he did not.

Now I began to understand what God meant when He said, "It is time to put off the reproach of Eve." Adam was the one who first placed the reproach on her. When God came to the garden and asked Adam why he had eaten the fruit, Adam said, "It was that woman you gave to be with me—she made me do it," knowing very well that was not the full truth. It was a half-truth. He became an accuser, testifying against the woman he had loved and cherished as his own flesh and bone. Discord had been sown between the man and woman, resulting in jealousy, fear and mistrust.

It has been that way ever since. The struggle between Adam and Eve goes on today in marriage and in the body of Christ. A spirit of competition flourishes between men and women even though they love each other. It is time to stop the subtle power plays, grappling and competing. We must begin to reach out in love to strengthen, encourage and hold up one another.

Where do you begin? Let me offer some practical suggestions.

At the head of the list is this: learn to trust again. Adam and Eve were torn apart by fear. Since then, men and women have been afraid to be vulnerable to one another. At times, some of us may *say* we're willing to trust, but there's a difference between saying it and meaning it.

Not long ago, I spoke on the subject of women in

leadership at a conference on the West Coast. Afterwards a woman approached me with a look of concern. She said, "My husband's a pastor, and he says he knows God wants to use me in some important roles in our church and community. But when I begin to step out and become active, he starts to act defensive. He's suddenly on guard."

I had to fight from smiling as I listened to her dilemma. How well I knew what she was talking about. For instance, John likes to cook because he enjoys eating food his way—with oregano and garlic and other spices and herbs. Since I don't fix food that way, he even prefers to cook—when no one else is around. But if we're having company, things are different. Then John likes to put his feet up and have me serve coffee, because tradition says man is supposed to be waited on hand and foot in his home. I understand this and I am willing to bless him in this way. He enjoys it and we both laugh about it later.

For his part, John is my biggest "fan." He sees potential in me that I don't see. He encourages me—even pushes me at times. People see the woman in the pulpit, the woman on television, the woman speaking at conventions and assume that I surely must be bold and aggressive. They don't see the woman who is totally dependent on God. When I would hesitate or even doubt myself—it is John who encourages me. He tells me to reach out beyond what I have ever achieved before, not to be afraid of a few mistakes, not to be afraid to lose, because fear will stop me from trying. He tells me to shoot for the moon and at least land on the stars. He knows his strengths and mine; he knows his weaknesses and mine. We draw on each other. We balance each other.

Balance results from trust. An amazing thing would happen in the church if we stopped trying to push ourselves into areas where we have no strength or calling or business. What power would result if men and women in the body of Christ would stop knocking each other down and start lifting each other up.

One day God spoke to my heart saying, "One of the greatest victories you and your husband will know is when you discern how Satan tries to anger you one with another." It was a real revelation to me and I realized how true it is. We can weather the attacks from without, but when we attack each other we lose out with God.

Among the things I told the pastor's wife at the conference was to pray for her husband. Reassure him that you love him and regard him as head of the house. Build him up so that he feels no danger of losing you. Then wait on the Lord; He will open doors for you at the right time. If you strive to keep your relationship with your husband strong and loving, he will be glad to see God blessing and using your life.

Second, as you step into a leadership role, be careful to continue your feminine role as well. Some women think that becoming a leader means that they no longer have responsibilities at home. They develop an attitude that serving their children and husband is somehow demeaning. I consider it a blessing to be both a wife and a mother. It is challenging and rewarding to me as a woman. Also I feel it is a good testimony before the church and the world to have all my bases covered. I can do well in these God-given roles and at the same time fulfill my calling in God.

Let's take this idea a step further. Don't be afraid of

your femininity. Women are gifted with intuitiveness. We are sensitive to people and often see right to the heart of a matter without being told the details. Learn to use this gift wisely. Grow in discernment about how to share your insight with others.

There is a third area we can work on in gaining the trust of others: Know the boundaries and guidelines set for you and live within them, remembering there are no short cuts in God.

I have known people—both men and women—who have a call to leadership but feel time is running out for them and they decide to rewrite the rule book. Suddenly they become unteachable; they think they are above all limitation or guidance or counsel. I have learned a secret I'll share by way of a brief personal anecdote.

When I was still single, I traveled with a group of Christians to a big conference of Pentecostal churches in Jamaica. Several others in the group, including a husband and wife team, were evangelists, besides myself. The Jamaicans welcomed us joyfully.

We arrived just in time for the two final nights of the meeting. An invitation was extended to the leader of our group to pick a speaker from among us for their final great service. He explained that I was an evangelist, and also the young couple with us were evangelists. Politely, the word came back that a woman had never spoken to their main island convention before.

Things were left rather indefinite. As the service began, I was informed that I would be given five minutes that night to testify. At once, I decided I would take only *three* minutes. Now here is the secret. Never go beyond what you have been asked to do. Never presume to be more *led* than the one in charge. They expect a woman to take advantage.

When my time came, I got up, shared a passage from Isaiah that had been made real to my heart, delivered my points—bam! wham!—and sat down. The leaders' mouths were hanging open. The service moved right along, but within 10 minutes a message came to me from the conference heads: Would I please consider preaching the following night? I learned a valuable secret that night, and it has never failed to work in my behalf.

When someone in authority gives you an inch, you never take a mile. You don't even have to take the whole inch. Take less than you are given and do *better* with it. What a surprise and what a breath of fresh air when we prefer our brethren.

Leaders must always be aware that they are working off the trust of others. If God has called and enabled you to be a leader, you must be aware of the responsibilities that go with that position. Others will look to you for counsel and direction. Your own life must become as an open book that others can see and read. Often you may feel you've given your all—only to find God would have you to encourage and lift up yet another of His precious flock. Rejoice that you're counted worthy and trust Him for the wisdom and strength for each task.

Being in a position of leadership has its own special rewards. You will be amazed at the paths that open before you. Your success doesn't depend on another's opinion of you nor on outward trappings, mannish attitudes or a polished presentation. It depends on your heart attitude, your personal relationship with God, and His anointing upon your life and ministry.

One person we often overlook in our quest for ministry, especially ministry in a church, is the pastor's wife. Always be mindful that she is the "first lady" of the church. Too often women make the mistake of seeking their pastor's advice on everything from child-rearing to marital problems to what flavor cake to bake for a church supper and totally ignore the pastor's wife. The point is that your most important ally can be your pastor's wife. It takes so little effort to seek her help, guidance and suggestions—to let her know that you value her and her giftedness too. The pastor and his wife are gifts to the church they serve. As you honor and esteem them, God will bless you.

I share these thoughts to encourage you in your call as a leader. The blessings far outweigh the struggles. If you are still unsure of your leadership role, or if you are struggling just now, I can tell you from much experience..."Humble yourselves therefore under the mighty hand of God, that He may exalt you in due time."

Chapter
SEVEN

WHOLENESS

Much is being written today about women and self-image, women and self-acceptance, women and fulfillment. We in the church ought to be getting the message that there has been a deep wound in the spirit of all womankind. But, even as I write, I know we are in the days when that wound is being healed. Women under God's sovereign direction are beginning to move into co-dominion, ruling at the side of their men, as kings and priests together in this exciting generation. God wants women to know strength and health and blessing such as no woman since Eve has experienced.

One of the first blessings coming to women is the healing of our wounded spirits. Low self-esteem and broken self-images have crippled so many of us for too long. How will that healing come about? And what are the blessings we can expect?

To begin, we listen in the quiet of our hearts for that sure call of God. As I search the Scriptures, I understand that real calls first happen privately, between God and the individual. The manner in which God calls the individual is personal, tailored to that person's heart and ears and deepest needs.

Today I know of many women (and men, too) who run from meeting to meeting hoping to "get a word" from somebody. Some are always looking for one more prophecy that will tell them "for sure" they have heard from God.

As I have already alluded, when I was very young, I knew God had spoken to my heart about my life's work. And though, as a girl, I really did not know why, I felt clearly that I was never to ask anyone else's opinion about it. It was something that was settled between God and me. Now I understand why. Over the years people have blessed me, and I've said amen. They've also cursed me, and I've just said amen to that, too. Because the foundation of my life is not built on man's view of me, but on God's.

What a tremendous blessing—the first and best blessing for anyone—to know that the God of the universe, Creator of stars and galaxies, *accepts* you and has marked you for some work, great or small, in His vast plan. As you become settled with the fact that God accepts you, you suddenly find that you accept yourself. You come to peace with the fact that you may be leading multitudes to Christ, or you may be teaching a few men and women in a Bible study, or you may be the Sunday school superintendent—but you are the important person in the very special niche that God carved out for you. No one else, in all God's plan, can fill that niche the way you can. You are His first choice; anyone else would be a stand-in. You are not taking someone else's place; God has given you your own place in His plan. How humbling, and how awesome!

The second blessing is related: the joy that comes when others recognize God's calling on you.

Now I've just said that the first wellspring of peace and healing comes from knowing God accepts you, and therefore you can accept yourself. But that certainly does not mean that we shouldn't be open to the confirming acceptance that comes from the recognition given us by others. God fashioned the body of Christ to be this wonderful support community. Relationships take on a new meaning. You find yourself feeling connected, not alone.

Beyond this acceptance by others is a third joy—that of actually ministering to people. There is a solidness, a confidence that comes when you know that God is actually using you. You start your days with expectancy because you don't know what God may use you for next.

Once when I was just beginning my ministry, my pastor made a comment about me to my best friend: "She will never make it in the ministry." When asked why, he replied, "For two reasons: first, she is a woman. Second, there are men who are better preachers than she is and they can't make it because of finances."

I heaved a sigh of relief, thinking, If those are his only reasons, I'm OK. I had long since settled it with God about being a woman, and God had spoken to my heart about finances. He said, *If you don't get what you thought you would get, you didn't need it. If you get more than you expected, don't get excited, you're going to need it.* I've never seen it fail. When a larger sum than expected came in, there was soon a place where it was urgently needed. All my needs and a lot of my wants have been abundantly supplied as I have looked to God as my source.

I have learned to depend on God's presence and the anointing of the Holy Spirit when I minister. One night just before I was to speak in the service, I sought God for the anointing. I was dry as a stick. I couldn't feel anything and I was beginning to panic on the inside.

Oh, God, I prayed, *anoint me. I can't go out there without the sense of Your power.*

In my heart, clear as a bell, I heard God say, *Do you want it now or when you get up to preach?*

Clearly God was teaching me something I needed to know, not only for this one service but for the future. In faith I went. And God met me there, right at the point of my need. When it was time to preach, the sense of the Holy Spirit's presence was so strong that my spirit leaped within me. Needless to say the word flowed with power.

On another occasion, I was not only *feeling* "out of it"; I *was* out of it. I was sick. Very sick. I was supposed to be leading a revival in a church in Victoria, Texas. When I stood up on the platform, I felt so weak that I thought I might fall down. As they introduced me, I stood and told myself that the least I could do for these good folks was to stand up straight, smile, and at least try to look as if I was going to make it through to the altar call!

As I made that one weak step, when I gave God the very best I had to offer—which didn't feel like very much—I heard His voice within me say, *The same spirit that raised Christ from the dead dwells in your mortal body—and I'm going to quicken your body right now.*

In a split second the anointing hit me—in the space of a heartbeat and a footstep. When I reached the pulpit, I knew I was supposed to put aside the notes I had in my Bible. I delivered a message by the Holy Spirit's revelation from start to finish. The Spirit flowed through me in spite of my physical limitations.

Those experiences reminded me of that poor widow who had so little to offer to the prophet, but she gave anyway. When she faithfully returned to her grain barrel, she found that God replenished her supply every time. That's the way it's been for me. Just when I think I have little or nothing at all left to give, I go back to my heavenly Father's rich storehouse and find that in my weaknesses and lack He willingly gives me power and abundance. I have the joy of knowing beyond the shadow of a doubt that the source of strength is really God Himself, not my emotions or some exuberance I've drummed up.

Once in great weariness of spirit, mind and body I told God, "I've given you the best years of my life." I was feeling a little bit sorry for myself. The answer quickly came back, *That's what I want, the best you have to offer—and I will give you My best.* When I look at my husband and daughter and the great church God has blessed us to pastor, I know He has truly given me the best. In fact, there are times I can scarcely imagine it; God uses *me*! I don't know why or how—but I'm not going to waste a lot of time worrying over it. I just want to be His willing vessel, no matter what it takes, no matter what the cost.

I believe very strongly that a fourth joyous blessing that will come to women who step out in leadership is a new sense of unity in their marriage.

It would seem just the opposite: that the husband-wife relationship is in grave danger when a woman starts to "assert" any authority. Let me give you some reasons why this does not have to be the case.

First of all, most of the women I've known who have become leaders in any sense immediately understand what their husbands have gone through for years. Being a leader, having to sit through meetings and trying to reach agreement among those you're working with is tough business. The responsibilities are far greater than the lay person can imagine. It's not all glory. It's work. If you've wondered for years why your husband does things a certain way or holds certain views, you will quickly find out when you step into any kind of leadership role.

Of course, this is a growing process for all couples. Though John and I have ministered together for years, sharing the same pulpit at church and the same pot of soup at home, I have always made it clear that on both fronts he is the real "chief." As an "Indian," I often had difficulty understanding some of his motivations.

For instance, when a service is over, the last person prayed for and the last amen said, I'll have on my hat and coat and be headed out the door like a shot. John, however, will stand there no matter how long somebody wants to talk to him. After many evening services, I've sat and watched through the rain-splattered windshield as he stands in the cold talking to someone who has "just one more thing to say." All the while I'd think, Can't it wait?

But just recently, as I've stepped out more on my own—and especially in starting the Women in Leadership ministry—I've come to appreciate my husband more than ever. At a recent meeting in Denver, God helped both John and me to gain a deeper and closer relationship. The meeting had been about Christian groups coming together in a new unity, and many couples who minister together were in attendance. At one point, a prophecy came forth, in words I too had been sensing in my spirit, and it hit me like wildfire.

The word that came was this: "As you go from this place, a restoration will come about between you and your spouse. Husbands reconciled with wives and wives with husbands. For the church has been in turmoil and relationships and homes have been broken because you were not healed yourself and could not bring healing to My people. But I am going to heal your relationship with your spouse as a token of what is to come."

John and I have always thought our relationship was pretty good. When we had tension or disagreements we only needed to get away together for a few days and everything seemed to work out. But when God speaks, things can only get better. There has truly been a change in our relationship. We have noticed a new tolerance, more patience and longsuffering toward one another. We have become more "elastic" with each other, making more allowances for each other, preferring one another more than ever before. Whose marriage could not use more of all those things? With my new leadership role, and with the work of the Holy Spirit, I understand John more. And I love him more than ever before.

A fifth blessing we can expect in leadership is the joy of producing good fruit. We think of preaching to multitudes, seeing hundreds of repentant sinners marching down the aisles to receive Christ. I have had the privilege of speaking to large gatherings in person and to multitudes via television. But nothing compares to seeing the fruit of my obedience to God borne in the life of my daughter, Robin Anne.

You may think or have been taught that a woman's family suffers when she reaches beyond her motherly role and takes on a calling. Answering God's call never means forsaking the natural duties of a wife and mother. Certainly, some women have forsaken their families—and so have many men—in answering a call to ministry. They give their lives for the "unsaved multitudes" but don't have the time of day for their own children. Those stories are tragic and heartbreaking. Don't let your story be that of a broken home or children who stray simply because you were too busy handling the problems of the world to be interested in theirs.

However, I know firsthand that when you, in faith, step into leadership God has ordained, your children can and will be blessed. We often overlook the divine destiny that God has in store for our children. (For a more complete study of this subject, you might wish to read my book, *Marking Your Children for God*.)

Many Christian parents I know have little faith that they will be able to lead their own children to Christ. They hope against hope that their children will ultimately choose God. They grab onto one verse out of the whole Bible upon which they base their children's future: "Train up a child in the way he should go: and when he is old he will not depart from it" (Prov. 22:6).

That's a wonderful verse. But it's future-tense faith, not present-tense faith. It speaks about the adulthood of our children. Many see in it an elastic clause that allows for their children to be hostile and rebellious toward God but suggests they will return to the faith

87

later.

Perhaps so, but we can expect to see the fruit of faith and godliness in our children *now*. Let's re-examine a verse we looked at earlier in another context: "And it shall come to pass...that I will pour out my spirit upon all flesh; and your sons and your daughters shall prophesy..." (Joel 2:28).

Your sons and daughters shall prophesy! They shall exhibit the gifts and fruit of God's Holy Spirit! There are other promises:

Lo, children are an heritage of the Lord: and the fruit of the womb is His reward. As arrows are in the hand of the mighty man; so are children of the youth. Happy is the man that hath his quiver full of them: They shall not be ashamed, but they shall speak with the enemies in the gate.

(Ps. 127:3-5)

These verses mean much more than "Happy is the man who has a lot of children." It says children are "an heritage." People spend their time worrying about IRAs, second homes, trust funds and savings accounts to provide "an heritage" for their children. There's nothing wrong with that. But the Bible says we can *invest* in our children. *They* are God's treasure. They are *our* heritage.

How do we invest—how do we mark our children for God? By example and by commitment.

I once saw a television commercial that warned against the dangers of smoking. It showed a father and son walking together, skipping stones on a lake, laughing, enjoying each other. Then they sat down under a tree, and the father lit up a cigarette. The little boy, following the father's example, picked up a twig and pretended to light up too. The message was obvious. He was following his father's example.

As Christian leaders, as women who would wisely rule over our own houses, we must remember how much of an impression we are always making on our children while we are "about the Lord's business." Ladies, if you want to know what you sound like, listen to the way your daughter talks to her dolls, or the way your older children boss around the younger ones. They sound so much like us that it's scary!

Up to a certain age, children think their parents are the greatest people in the world. For most of us, when we were small, our parents could do no wrong. Even when, as teenagers or young adults, we vow to do certain things differently from how our parents did them, we often hear the same words coming from our own lips, or see ourselves react just the way Dad or Mom did.

A man once came to us for counsel about his terrible relationship with his son. The man had allowed himself a lot of "slack" in his spiritual walk, and he came weeping and repenting. He said, through tears, "I was sitting with my boy and we were trying to deal with his problem, and all of a sudden God spoke to me. He said, 'The reason your son has that rebellion in him is because he got it from you.' Everything my son was doing I saw in myself."

That's true, but it's also true that we can develop godly habits in our children: prayer, repentance, a love for church and the Word of God, and expectation of God's provision and intervention in their lives.

Example must be turned into commitment. I have learned a great deal from the story of Hannah, the mother of the prophet Samuel. Her story came to me at a time when I was myself asking God many questions about my own child. Even though John and I were "training up" Robin in godly ways, I wondered, What about her salvation? The Bible says, "You must be born again," and we know that salvation is not inherited. That was when I rediscovered Hannah and her marvelous life of commitment.

Hannah dedicated her son to the Lord even before he was born. Then she weaned him, clothed him, loved him—and brought him to the house of the Lord. She was saying, "You shall serve God because I made a covenant, not because you made one. You are God's. This is where you belong." There Samuel was raised, and there he learned what it was like to serve God and wait on Him even before he had a living heart-faith of his own. "Now Samuel did not yet know the Lord, nor was the word of the Lord yet revealed to him" (1 Sam. 3:7).

When God did speak to Samuel, the young man did not even recognize His voice. Old Eli had to tell him, "Go back and lie down and listen. God wants to have a personal relationship with you."

This story comforted me greatly. About the time I was rediscovering it, Robin asked, "Mother, was I raised in church?"

I had to laugh. "Robin," I said, "you might say you were raised on the pew!"

Robin came to church for the first time when she was four weeks old. She's been there ever since. When she was 3 years old, John was taking her to a vacation Bible school. As they walked together, she held one of her Dad's hands with one hand and her little New Testament in the other. She looked up at him innocently and asked, "Am I preaching today?"

Barely able to stifle his laughter, John said soberly, "No. I think they've already taken care of that. All you have to do is go and sit there."

For years after that, Robin was fascinated by the baptism ceremony. Many times she would ask if she too could be baptized "like everyone else." We knew she was not ready, and we gently said, "Not yet."

Then one day, when she was only 7, she came to us, with a different light in her eyes." She said—she did not ask—"Next Sunday I'm going to be baptized." We knew that she had had a spiritual "dawning." Again, I did not respond, but thought, We'll see.

That next Sunday morning, she went off to children's church as usual. Then at the end of the main service, when we normally baptize, she came into the sanctuary and went up to one of the older ladies who was waiting for her. Watching her, I realized that she had already made all the arrangements. She was on her way back to the dressing room before I could decide whether or not to stop her.

John was baptizing that morning, and the look on his face when Robin stepped out was priceless. He was beaming, and I was beginning to choke up. We flashed a glance at each other—and we knew this was right.

When John lowered our little girl under the water, my heart was bursting. And when she came up—! Her hands were in the air, and the power of the Holy Spirit fell on her. My little girl stood there laughing and praising God in *tongues*.

That morning was just the beginning of the most precious fruit I have ever harvested as a parent and as a leader in God's kingdom. Since then, Robin has continued to walk with the Lord—certainly not without the normal teenage struggles and questions—but her heart is toward God. That is what counts.

Truly, God is fulfilling His promises of old in this very hour. For our sons and daughters will prophesy and see visions. The turning of their lives toward God will be part of the greatest heritage that we as leaders of the renewal movement will leave to future generations.

What does the future hold? So far, we have looked back in time and considered what we can do in this present day to bring women back to the place of co-dominion with men that God intends them to have. We need to catch another glimpse of the future. We need to look forward to the new day that is already dawning. The message that God is bringing forth in this hour is powerful. He is restoring unity and harmony between men and women—husbands and wives—brother and sister in Christ. What a glorious time to be living. How blessed and privileged you and I are.

Chapter
EIGHT

WOMEN RESTORED

Today we are living in a marvelous age in the history of the church. God is revealing Himself in a dimension in which no other generation has known Him. Revival, renewal and restoration are taking place throughout the church as God prepares us for the return of our Lord Jesus Christ.

From the early days of this present movement of the Holy Spirit, as far back as the 1800s, God began to call forth women leaders. God raised up Hannah Whitall Smith—when her husband failed in ministry—to preach throughout Europe and the United States. Though few today realize it, she was an early advocate of temperance and of women's rights to vote and to receive higher education (both of which are now all but taken for granted!). Her books have influenced millions. In the early 1900s, Aimee Semple McPherson emerged from the Azusa Street revival as a leader, founding the Foursquare denomination and having a worldwide impact.

CBS News has reported that enrollment at schools of

religion, seminaries and biblical studies programs is increasing rapidly. An unprecedented 25 percent of those enrolling are women. A door is opening, and some are hearing the call.

God has done this! Why do we refuse and neglect our heritage and calling?

First, because much of the church is still bound by the traditions of men. Today the church must arise and understand that women stand equal before God.

God's patterns of authority for the home and marriage are clear: God is over the man; the man is over the woman and children. Break that pattern and God will break you. If you do not follow God's way, you won't make it any other way.

But when husbands and wives stand before God, they are joint heirs because of the power that is in the precious blood of Jesus Christ. When the last trumpet sounds and mortality puts on immortality, I will drop off this robe of clay. Male and female, bond and free, Jew and Greek will all be revealed for what they are. Right now, the real us is jumping up and down on the inside crying, "Abba, Father!"

Not everyone is happy about the restoration of women. Satan is furious! He is the enemy of all women and especially the godly woman. Why?

Have you heard of the feminist movement? The feminists are after much more than legal rights and equal pay for equal work. Feminists have already had a strong influence on the church. They have pushed some churches to stop referring to God as Father, He, Him. They say that is sexist. Instead, they refer to God as Father/Mother, or even worse, just Mother. That opens the way to the worship of the old pantheon of deities that our God, the God of the Bible, abhors.

These feminists want to hold onto the "right" to sacrifice their unborn children on the altars of self-indulgence and convenience. Millions of babies are being killed in abortion each year. Anyone who opposes the feminists' causes is decried as fanatical and un-American.

I am not exaggerating. Gloria Steinem, one of the most influential and outspoken leaders of the feminist movement, has said that feminism is the path to humanism, and that humanism is their goal.

The *Humanist Manifesto* states that a goal of the humanist movement is to discredit religion which is based on the Bible. One of the humanists' most familiar quotes is this: "No deity can save us; we must save ourselves." A 1973 report on the goals of the National Organization of Women stated: "Biblical religion is seen as an enemy in light of the enslavement of body and mind which the church has historically imposed upon women. We demand that the seminaries immediately stop and repudiate their propagation of sexist male supremacy doctrines."

Feminism is a counterfeit of what God intends to do by restoring the godly woman. For we are not feminists. We are not humanists. We are women who believe in God and in His Word. We must always be clear on those points.

Satan also hates the restoration of women because he knows this is a missing piece in the full restoration of the church.

Why has Satan kept women down for so many centuries? Because he heard God say in the Garden of Eden that the seed of the woman would bruise his head. Satan knows that women are a link to the church's power.

What role of power can women play today? I believe that women are going to be used to bring unity in the body of Christ. God spoke to my heart very clearly about this one day recently.

I had a vision of something like an oxford shoe, un-laced and wide open. Then a hand began threading a cloth lace through the holes, back and forth from one side to the other. At last, the whole thing was laced together, and then the hand gave one simple tug, and the whole thing drew together perfectly.

And God's voice in my heart said, *That is the role that godly women are going to play in My church.*

I thought, How can this be?

At once, an idea came to mind. Suppose women in local churches started inviting their pastors and other men to get together for fellowship and prayer. It would not be a gathering with a heavy agenda, just Christian men coming together in a relaxed way to fellowship and learn to care for each other—hostessed by a godly woman who was praying for unity the whole time!

Suppose the wives of Christian leaders banded together, working behind the scenes to draw their husbands together. I began to see how, in a very sub-tle, feminine and influential way, women will bring Christians and their leaders together.

There is one very important key in all this: our heart attitude.

Christian woman, examine your heart. Quit trying to boss your husband. Quit trying to be his spiritual head even if you have a more active spiritual life at present. Christ is the head of your husband.

Ladies, I have news for you, something my mother

told me a long time ago. She said, "Anne, your daddy won't listen to me. It's as if he can't hear me. I can say something to him, but he won't really hear it until it comes from someone else." I laughed—until the day I got married. Many of you women know exactly what I mean.

The point is, there is something peculiar about the way God fashioned a man's ears. They don't hear the voice of a bossy woman! That is right, for a woman is not to teach her husband; she is to honor and esteem him as the leader in the home. Just like Esther, your husband, "the king," will honor you.

But when Christian women begin to move in their beautiful role of bringing unity in the body of the Christ, something special will break forth on this land. There is a prophetic passage in the Song of Solomon which has long been interpreted as God's "love letter" to the church. The friends of the beloved exclaim, "Who is this that cometh up from the wilderness, leaning upon her beloved?" (Song 8:5).

When the godly woman begins to enter into co-dominion and leadership, she will not have to beat her own drum and toot her own horn. Someone else will do it for her! Godly men will recognize the ministries of godly women, and even the world will say, "Who is this coming up out of the wilderness?"

We women have been in a wilderness for a long time, but the time of our wilderness wanderings is at an end. Consider the story of Elijah when he went to visit a poor, widowed woman who was on the verge of starvation.

First, God sent Elijah to the brook, but the brook was dried up. Then God spoke to him and said, "Arise, get thee to Zarephath, which belongeth to Zidon, and dwell there: behold, I have commanded a widow woman there to sustain thee" (1 Kings 17:9).

When Elijah got there, the widow did not seem to know anything about his coming. She became somewhat indignant when Elijah suggested that she share her little bit of food with him. She had enough food for one last meal for herself and her son. After this they would starve.

She told Elijah that she did not have anything to give him. We might interpret her reply this way: "I am going to do what I have always been told to do—minister to my household. Don't ask anything more of me. I am not going to do anything else."

But Elijah spoke forth with the voice of God and revealed what was really the underlying problem. He said, "Fear not! Go and do what thou hast said, but first make a cake and minister to the man of God."

And I say to the women of God today, "Fear not!" Fear is one of the greatest cripplers of all women. It need not be a tool of the enemy any longer.

This is a new day. God has been teaching us for a long time, helping us learn how to get our lives in order, how to be godly women. He is not expecting perfection, just faithfulness in answering His call.

As America and the world face some of the darkest hours in human history, I say to you, woman of God: Now is the time to come forth and walk in the way of co-dominion which God has planned for you.

For even as the darkness swells, it is almost time for our Bridegroom to return to us. And then His everlasting light will break forth!

AFTERWORD

God has been speaking strongly to my heart about the restoration of women. Women have always had a solidifying effect on the family. Woman is the one who binds up the wounds, comforts, draws people together in warm relationships. Take woman out of the home and the home will crumble. A call to ministry is not a call to abandon the home.

But in this hour women will be used to bring unity in the body of Christ, to help heal and soothe, for Christ is returning for a bride "without spot or wrinkle" (Eph. 5:27).

Ever since I began writing this book astounding things have happened in the reconciliation of men and women in the church.

Recently, John and I attended a gathering of many independent charismatic ministries, college and parachurch groups. It was an important, even historic, gathering because the conference brought together groups that had been divided and out of fellowship with each other for years.

On the last night of the gathering, John spoke about the wonderful healings that were happening in the body of Christ, the unity and restoration that must surely be a blessing to God.

As he spoke, a remarkable thing happened. In the audience were two men of international stature who had taught for years that women were never to speak in public meetings, not even to exercise gifts of the Spirit. When they asked to be recognized from the floor, right at the end of John's teaching, I felt an electricity.

The first man said that, since he had separated himself from the mainstream of the charismatic movement nearly a decade ago, his greatest fear had been that God would move on and that he would not know it. I could feel the hearts of everyone present reaching out to embrace this brother anew.

And then the second man stood up. His first words gripped me. "I'm impressed with the ministries that are represented here. The people here are all visionaries. Doers.

"There is one 'stand' we've been known for," he continued, and I could feel something coming. "We've openly opposed women in ministry." There was a long pause, and the room was absolutely silent.

Then he turned, and even sitting in the back row I could tell he was looking straight at me. He raised his arm and pointed at me, and in as warm a voice as I could hope for, he said, "Anne Gimenez, I want you to know that I accept your ministry. I accept you in the body of Christ."

I was elated, and at the same time, embarrassed to be singled out, for there were other women with national ministries present. But later, when we were alone, John said to me, "You have no reason to be embarrassed. You don't see what he was really doing. You are one of the few women nationally known as a preacher. You have been in the forefront for years, paving the way for others. And so you're a representative. By accepting you, he was opening the way for others to come after you."

That is why I say, with great excitement and confidence, the godly woman is standing on the horizon. And both the world and the church are saying, "Who is this? What is this new move of God's Spirit?" And soon they will know that we are just resuming our place in God's kingdom.

We are the "Esther generation." It is for this hour that God is calling us. And God has given us feminine skills, talents, abilities and wisdom for a purpose. As we obey God, our sons and daughters will follow in our footsteps and walk the godly path. For we women are a key to what God wants to do in this hour. We are God's secret weapon.

So, like Esther, I say to you, "Polish the silver and prepare the feast. There is going to be a celebration!"

RECOMMENDED READING

Allison, Joseph. *Setting Goals That Count: A Christian Perspective*. Chosen Books, 1985. ($4.95)

Ecker, Richard E. *The Stress Myth: Why the Pressures of Life Don't Have to Get You Down*. InterVarsity Press, 1985. ($4.95)

Eims, Leroy. *Laboring in the Harvest: A Practical Approach to Reviving Christ's Church and Accomplishing His Great Commission*. Navpress, 1985. ($4.95)

Hepburn, Daisy. *Lead, Follow, or Get Out of the Way: A New Look at Servant-Leadership Roles for Women*. Regal Books, 1982. ($4.95)

*Hospital Visitation: A Guide to Visiting the Sick and Elderly.*U.S.A. Hospital Christian Fellowship Inc., 1985. ($4.95)

Inrig, Gary. *A Call to Excellence: Understanding Excellence God's Way*. Victor, 1985. ($4.50)

Swindoll, Charles. *Leadership: Influence That Inspires*. Word, 1985. ($7.95)

Williams, June A. *Strategy of Service: Touching the Hurting and Needy of Your Community*. Zondervan, 1984. ($5.95)

OTHER PUBLICATIONS OF INTEREST FROM STRANG COMMUNICATIONS COMPANY

Youth Pastor's Handbook
A unique reference tool for busy youth leaders. This three-ring binder is full of practical and helpful information to make your youth meetings and projects successful. $25.00

Mountain-Moving Motivation
by Karl Strader
Discover how you can harness the power of God to move those mountains in your life. Written in Pastor Strader's own easy-to-read style. $3.95

Solving the Ministry's Toughest Problems, Vol. I & II
These practical resource books answer the questions most commonly asked by church leaders. Each volume has over 400 pages of solutions to the toughest ministry questions. $24.95 each. Both volumes $35.00

Available at your Christian bookstore or from:
Creation House
190 N. Westmonte Drive
Altamonte Springs, FL 32714